PENGUIN BOOKS
Pennies from Heaven

Frances and Philip Stone work in book publishing
in New York. After their own struggle with infertility, they now have two children.

Pennies from Heaven

✳

101 Meditations
for Couples Trying
to Get Pregnant

Frances and Philip Stone

PENGUIN BOOKS

PENGUIN BOOKS

Published by the Penguin Group

Penguin Putnam Inc., 375 Hudson Street,
New York, New York 10014, U.S.A.
Penguin Books Ltd, 27 Wrights Lane,
London W8 5TZ, England
Penguin Books Australia Ltd, Ringwood,
Victoria, Australia
Penguin Books Canada Ltd, 10 Alcorn Avenue,
Toronto, Ontario, Canada M4V 3B2
Penguin Books (N.Z.) Ltd, 182–190 Wairau Road,
Auckland 10, New Zealand

Penguin Books Ltd, Registered Offices:
Harmondsworth, Middlesex, England

First published in Penguin Books 1998

10 9 8 7 6 5 4 3 2 1

Copyright © Frances Stone and Philip Stone, 1998
All rights reserved

LIBRARY OF CONGRESS
CATALOGING IN PUBLICATION DATA
Stone, Frances.
Pennies from heaven: 101 meditations for
couples trying to get pregnant/Frances and Philip
Stone.
  p. cm.
  ISBN 0 14 02.5529 X (pbk.)
  1. Infertility—Popular works. 2. Fertility,
Human—Popular works. 3. Self-help
techniques. I. Stone, Philip. II. Title.
RC889.S75 1998
616.6'92—dc21   97–45615

Printed in the United States of America
Set in Sabon
Designed by Virginia Norey

Except in the United States of America, this book is
sold subject to the condition that it shall not, by way
of trade or otherwise, be lent, re-sold, hired out, or
otherwise circulated without the publisher's prior
consent in any form of binding or cover other than
that in which it is published and without a similar
condition including this condition being imposed on
the subsequent purchaser.

For all the babies yet to be born.

✳

There was a disturbance in my heart, a voice that spoke there and said, I want, I want, I want! It happened every afternoon, and when I tried to suppress it it got even stronger. . . . It never said a thing except I want, I want, I want!

—Saul Bellow,
Henderson the Rain King

Acknowledgments

The authors wish to thank their editor, Mindy Werner, and agent, Carla Mayer Glasser, for their dedication to this project. We would also like to thank the many friends and strangers who shared their stories with us, as well as those who helped confirm the accuracy of medical information. In addition, we wish to thank J. R. McGregor for his invaluable help in researching quotes, especially the story of Job.

✲

Introduction

Everybody knows someone who is trying to get pregnant. Your neighbors down the street are trying. So are some of your friends from work, or maybe a friend of a friend. And so are you. It's endless and it's heartbreaking if it doesn't happen as soon as you decide you want a child. Why can't you get pregnant? What if you *never* get pregnant? Everyone else is pregnant; everyone else already has a baby, or several children. Why you? Why can't you, now that you finally *want* to settle down into the patterns of family and children? It seems so unfair.

There are levels to the stages of disappointment. The menstrual period that suddenly seems so regular, the physical relief that was so welcome during the years when the last thing you wanted was to get pregnant, now becomes a cruel process, draining away more than the lifeblood that could have become something else. . . . Or the concerned questions from your mother or your best friend. You can feel the tension when they *don't* ask—after so many months, most friends simply stop asking, and in some ways this makes it more difficult. It's all you can think about, this business of getting pregnant, and you can't discuss it with those who love you for fear of jinxing it, for fear of scaring your own mother with your despair and loneliness, or offending your friend with your fundamental lack of faith in her words, which were intended only to make you feel better. You don't feel better. You feel worse. You just want to cry.

So instead of putting your shaken faith in the people who love you best, you put all your hopes in the advice of doctors, in the endless tests, the procedures, and the statistics. And it's the statistics that get you as you are lying in bed trying to relax. It probably won't happen, you think. The numbers are against me. I shouldn't get my hopes up.

This book is intended for those many couples who have just about had it with the doctors and the statistics, the concerned friends and family members who have already produced their 2.2 children, the rabbis and priests who can't possibly know the depths of your despair or who are critical of the selfishness of your desire. It's for the many who pick fights with their spouses, who pour themselves into their work, who can't see the forest for the trees because they've been looking and hoping for it for just too long. The thing is, we never do lose hope or faith. It's always there, lurking in our hearts. We just sometimes lose track of it.

*

We tried to get pregnant for so long we almost—almost —gave up on conceiving naturally. We tried everything you are supposed to try. We did the tests. We anxiously charted temperatures every morning. We watched the calendar, and when the crucial days approached, we brought out the ovulation kit—and a good bottle of wine for extra help. We tried to relax. We tried to think about romance. We *tried* to enjoy ourselves—and sometimes we did. As the months wore on, though, it became more difficult, and before long we began to wonder whether we would ever really be parents.

A book such as this would have helped us immensely and our hope is that it will help you. Although there is somewhat of a progression to the entries, this book is meant to be dipped into rather than read front to back. Pick it up the next time your period comes, or when you have to be out of town on business during those crucial three days. Browse a little, until you find something that strikes a chord. If you have a specific issue, whether it be envy or fear or a low sperm count, we hope you find what you're looking for. (We also hope the book will be useful to those experiencing secondary—or even tertiary—infertility.) The quotes and thoughts are intended to comfort and cajole, provide an occasional laugh, some practical information, and remind you that you are not alone in your quest. We didn't write each meditation together, but rather alternated entries, a device which we hope makes the book useful to both males and females. Nor is this little book intended to be the complete guide to solving your infertility problems. Rather, think of it as a source of inspiration or solace, always there for you to turn to when no one else is around—or when you don't want anybody else to be around. While we realize each "meditation" can't possibly appeal to everyone with an infertility problem, we have tried to be as sensitive as possible to the range of emotions out there. In the end, we wrote from our hearts.

Our own story does have a happy ending, although it took several years from start to finish and many, many days of worry and anxiety, of anger, of hope and faith, of arguments and tears and kisses. Eventually, and purely by chance, we conceived. It felt like a miracle, which of course it is. Whether by it's by sheer luck or with the help of high-tech science, *it will happen for you, too.*

Pennies from Heaven

*

Ev'ry time it rains it rains
pennies from Heaven.
Don't you know each cloud contains
pennies from Heaven?

—*Johnny Burke,*
"Pennies from Heaven"

★

We all know the concept. Every cloud has a silver lining. It sounds trite, and it is until you actually find yourself hopelessly surrounded by a permanent dark cloud. Not being able to get pregnant easily is a depressing shock to even the most optimistic. And since most of us who are childless and over thirty-five are naturally inclined to at least a moderate dose of pessimism, sometimes you need a little help. Pennies from Heaven? Well, maybe it's a stretch, but it's the thought that counts, right? At the very least, it's a happy thought to keep you going. Or get you going. Things might not be looking up for you right now, but they will. This refrain from 1936 lifted the mood of a generation coming out of the Depression. Let it help you.

I get so frustrated, it seems there is nothing out there about male infertility!

—infertility newsgroup participant on the Internet

True. Books abound on the subject of female reproductive systems and childbearing issues. But there is nothing around for the man. Perhaps it is thought that men care less, that children are a topic more appropriate to women, that we just don't care.

As unemotive as many men are, and as hard a time as we have being open about and discussing private, personal issues (how many close friends can a man truly count up?), the fact is that, when it comes to kids, men feel as strongly as women. We just display our feelings in a different way. And on the issue of the ability to conceive, we must be able to talk about it with someone besides our local (un)friendly doctor. The best source for men, most likely, is other men. We have to learn to open up to each other, to talk about our problems without shame. I think we'd be surprised at the number of men around us who are going through the same thing.

Not so long ago cancer was a forbidden issue. No one spoke of it; no one had support who was battling it. Reproductive problems, while far less consequential and tragic, are nowadays equally forbidden, especially among men. Well, open up! You might find it helpful to communicate via the Internet to express your feelings. Get the word out. You'll be surprised at the number of people who respond.

We are, perhaps, uniquely among the earth's creatures, the worrying animal.

—Lewis Thomas,
The Medusa and the Snail

So. It's natural to worry. It's our destiny. You've spent years trying to *not* get pregnant, anxiously fretting when your period was a few days late. Now you spend your days wracked with worry that you never will get pregnant. Everyone else in the universe will get pregnant except you. What if you worry so much you won't get pregnant even if you are able to? What if you get pregnant, but miscarry? What if you weren't *meant* to get pregnant? What if the abortion you had was your only chance? You drive yourself crazy with the "what ifs." Your friends will tell you not to worry and there will be days when you'll want to scream at them to shut up. It's normal. Try to relax. And try to not worry so much.

From the sperm's perspective, modern life abounds with perils.

—Lawrence Wechsler,
"Silent Sperm,"
The New Yorker

X-rays. Tobacco. Bad diet. Drugs of all kinds, including seemingly harmless antibiotics like penicillin and tetracycline. Marijuana. Tight underwear. Gas fumes (such as those found in garages or tunnels). Consumption of too much animal fat. It's a rough world out there—or in there—for sperm production. And given its importance, you'd think a man who wants to have children would work on these aspects of his life, all so easy to monitor and adjust, in order to maximize his chances of fertility.

Easier said than done, perhaps. But, with a minimum of effort, you can even the playing field and give your body a fighting chance to produce healthy sperm. Work on eating less meat and fatty foods. Is it so hard to have fruit juice for a while instead of a glass of bourbon? Do you *have* to get high? Any modifications of your own behavior—and these are all really, really easy to do—will do wonders. Both in the short term, as you will help increase your parenting probabilities, and in the long term, when you will notice a dramatically increased level of well-being and body happiness.

It is easier to resist at the beginning than at the end.

—*Leonardo da Vinci,*
The Notebooks

✳

All of us, at least initially, resist the idea that we might actually have to try to get pregnant. We like to think that conception is something that just happens, that *will* happen, once we are ready for it. Even after some months pass, and the cold possibility that we might have trouble conceiving starts to enter our consciousness, we still resist. It'll happen this month, we think.

Perhaps such resistance comes from some outdated perception that aided conception somehow isn't as "good" as one that occurs on its own. Or maybe it comes from an arrogance that you just shouldn't have to try that hard, that if you do, something's not right about it.

Something isn't right. If you want to get pregnant, stop resisting the initial tests or the sophisticated science of assisted reproduction. Your problem may be a simple one, or it may be frighteningly complex. Either way, get thee to a specialist.

Nothing can bring you peace but yourself.

—*Ralph Waldo Emerson,*
Essays

*

If we get pregnant, everything will be all right. If only we were pregnant. Things would be fine if we knew we were about to be parents.

It's easy to feel that life will get started only when something else happens. You wait, and wait, and wait, feeling that your life will get on track once the big event, whatever that is, takes place. But, as you know deep down, that's just not true. Try to stop thinking about the what-ifs. Make time for today. Life can be full, or it can be empty, but it's happening now, and it's the only life you have. Once you stop the waiting, you can really begin the living.

Love me tender, love me sweet,
Never let me go.

—*Elvis Presley,*
"Love Me Tender"

Let's be honest. Infertility takes a toll on romance. More often than not, as time goes on, making love or even just having fun sex becomes a thing of the past. The tests you have to take put a real chill on it, especially the post-coital. How romantic can it be when you've set your alarm so you can do it by 6:00 A.M. in order to be at your doctor's office by 8:00 and at work by 9:00? Or it might be the ovulation kit results: Okay honey, I know you're tired, but we've got to get busy—this *might* be the right time. Usually you manage to have a horrible fight just about midcycle. Romance? Love? Forget about it.

But over time you get the hang of it, and you are able to laugh, sometimes, and even to have fun. More important, you realize just how much you love each other, and how much you want a child, together, no matter how many obstacles you have to overcome. You are able to bond in a way you never would have otherwise. It's possible that if you had gotten pregnant right away, you would have missed the unique closeness that adversity has given you both—nor would you be as sure about your commitment to parenthood.

So remember how much you love your partner and your life together, whether you are able to conceive or not, and give each other all the tenderness you can.

All serious daring starts from within.

—Eudora Welty,
One Writer's Beginning

It is probably tempting, in the midst of all the anxiety you're encountering at home—tension with your mate, sadness about your lack of ability to conceive to date, with perhaps even a dash of performance anxiety—to remember that you weren't sure you really wanted to have children in the first place, and that things were much easier when it was just the two of you going out and having fun. Why wreck it now? Why not just go back to having fun, and see what happens? In the meantime, relax and don't worry about having children.

You've come a long way since the early days of your courtship. What you've embarked upon now has made you a person with much more depth to offer your partner. The decision to have children is momentous. It's also immensely liberating and exciting. You're going to be challenged as you never have been before, and you'll discover things about yourself—good things, strong things—that you never knew. Find the courage to grow, to embrace the world, to think beyond yourself. The resolve to achieve our hopes comes from within.

Time, that aged nurse,
Rocked me to patience.

—John Keats,
preface to Endymion

Patience is perhaps the most difficult virtue when you are trying to get pregnant, and time seems like your worst enemy. Time is what you feel you don't have. Ironically, time is what you *do* have. As the sayings go, you are never as old as you think you are and it is never too late. There are several ways to look at it. If you are thirty-five or younger, most doctors will tell you to try on your own for at least a year. You can help by trying to relax and find patience in simple mind-body therapies such as yoga and meditation. If you are older, or have been trying longer, or for whatever reasons are hopelessly worried about your ability to conceive, you can give yourself over to the miracles modern medicine offers couples who suffer from infertility. So many medical options are available today and so many more will be available in the future. Let time be your ally.

Life is the garment we continually alter, but which never seems to fit.

—David McCord,
Whereas to Mr. Franklin

*

The decision to marry, or to live with someone, is highly significant and takes a great deal of thought and soul-searching. And once that decision has been made and carried out, other choices come along: do we move apartments? Do we get a house? Do we want to change our jobs, or our diet? Large and small, whether our decisions involve vacations, choice of clothing, major purchases, or moral choices, we're always changing something in our lives and moving everything in a direction, forward or backward. It's the human need to change aspects of our lives continually. We never seem to sit still and enjoy what we have when we have it. The need to alter our circumstances probably keeps us alert and vital, growing constantly to adapt to new situations. But things never seem quite *there* yet. Do you know anyone whose life is in perfect order? Take a moment to think about what is good in your present life. Assess what those things are, and recognize how valuable they are to your stability. Savor constancy, if only for a day.

*No one can make you feel inferior
without your consent.*

—*Eleanor Roosevelt,*
This is My Story

Once you've decided you want to have children, nothing can make you feel more like a failure than not being able to conceive. This is even more the case when, for whatever reasons, you have put off having children until later. Conception seems like such a natural, easy thing; in evolutionary terms, reproduction is what we are made for. So when it doesn't happen right away, and then doesn't happen month after month after month, you do feel inferior. The pervasive feeling that something is wrong with you, and that the dreaded word "infertile" applies to more than just your reproductive organs, is dangerous territory. You start to see it, or feel it, in every question your mother asks, in every glance a young mother of three gives you. You feel that way seeing strangers on the subway, or walking past playgrounds. But while everything and everyone can make you feel this way, you are the only one who can conquer it. Don't give in. Take a deep breath and square your shoulders. Have faith in yourself.

Eighty percent of success is showing up.

—*Woody Allen*

*

Okay, the tests are no fun at all. Waiting around in a doctor's office, answering awkward questions, being made to undergo unpleasant exams—it's all too much. Is this really what you bargained for? Do you have to do this? Is it worth it?

As demeaning as the medical side of all this might feel, yes, you do need to do it. It's important to follow through, and really, it isn't the Spanish Inquisition. A few exams might turn up something that you can easily remedy with a prescription or a simple procedure. Or they might show that there's no problem at all, that you just need to be patient. Imagine your relief if you find out that's the case. Like so much of life, it may just be a question of timing. All things come to pass in their own season, as the Bible says, and conception is certainly no exception. Show up for the tests. Just do them. Your partner will feel like you're doing your part, and actually, so will you. What's important is that you're doing this together.

We haven't the time to take our time.

—Eugène Ionesco,
Exit the King

*

Family and friends love to counsel you to just give it
time. They mean well and in some respects they are right.
But that doesn't help how you *feel*. When the anxiety that
comes from each passing month threatens to overwhelm
you, it's time to get to work. Don't waste another minute
with your OB/GYN no matter how long you have been
going to him or her. If you are already in your thirties,
both you and your husband should go see a fertility expert.
Start asking around for recommendations, start interview-
ing doctors or clinics, and choose the one you are most
comfortable with. If you are not familiar with the basic
terminology, get yourself to the library. If you haven't yet,
you will need to proceed with a basic fertility workup, but
you can have several tests done around the same time.
Don't wait, for instance, for the results of ovulation hormone levels and X-rays before getting sperm counts and

motility reports. If your husband is dragging his feet, tell him to snap out of it. You need to work together on this, even if it is unpleasant or embarrassing. Antibodies can be a simple problem to correct, or one which can complicate other procedures; if your doctor doesn't suggest checking for them, request the test. Educate yourselves, read everything, talk to everyone you know who has suffered from infertility of any kind.

Get cracking.

The worst sin—perhaps the only sin—passion can commit, is to be joyless.

—Dorothy Sayers,
Gaudy Night

*

Well, in your life sex has certainly been treated differently lately, hasn't it? With the focus of lovemaking centered on conception, the whole experience can become quite mechanical and uninteresting, if not downright boring. Nothing will cut the mood faster than the sense that sex has to be done, and done now, quickly and efficiently. Come on, kid! Time to party!

If you can find any humor in the situation, by all means try to do so. Yes, the timing issue is a mood killer. And so is the relentlessness of going to bed just to conceive. If possible, take one minute to laugh about how boring, how beyond normality, how *silly* what you're doing is. A good laugh will help reduce the stress level of the moment. It will bring you both together, with a sense of sharing the silliness for a good reason. It will make you feel good about each other again. It may even kindle a twinkle in your eye. Being relaxed and comfortable with your partner will go a long way to making the joint effort feel shared, and pleasurable. Then, feel a sense of joy! And go to it!

I'm sure it wouldn't interest anybody
Outside of a small circle of friends.

—Phil Ochs,
"Outside of a Small Circle of Friends"

When you are in the midst of trying to get pregnant, month after month, it's difficult to remember that anybody cares besides you and your doctor. It's especially trying when the friends and family you *have* involved stop asking, or don't know what to say when you admit you got your period again. It's hard to break through the cocoon of your own sorrow and let them share it with you a little. It's hard to talk about it at all unless you're talking to somebody who is having the same problem.

But your situation *is* of interest to your friends. Don't add to your burden by keeping silent. Truly, talking about it isn't going to jinx the possibility of conception later in the month. Infertility is such a common problem these days almost everyone has either gone through it themselves or knows someone else who has. And their stories help: the friends who went through all the tests only to find out that nothing was wrong, but still couldn't conceive until after they did the GIFT program; the neighbors who were planning to adopt because tubal scarring made conception virtually impossible, yet are now four months pregnant; the acquaintance who took Pergonal and joyfully has twins. These stories do help. And sharing your experiences may in turn help someone else.

Praise the Lord and pass the ammunition.

—*Howell M. Forgy*

✳

No doubt there have been many times lately when you have reached the end of your rope. You've followed everyone's advice—and everyone has had a lot of advice to give. You've changed your diet, tried working on your mood, changed bedrooms (for the novelty of it). Yet all this hasn't added up to anything particularly different. Well, it may never. This is the time to buckle down, not grimly, but with renewed resolve. Yes, it *is* frustrating, and hard, and boring. But keep at it. The only way your hopes will come true is by trying, and trying, and trying again. There's no alternative. Take a deep breath, come to grips with the fact that, if you want this to happen for you, you'll have to do it yourself, and, at the risk of sounding like a cliché, find the inner strength to move forward to meet the challenge. Pass that ammunition! Take all the steps you feel you need to take, but keep at it!

I should have stood in bed.

—Joe Jacobs

✳

Jacobs (heavyweight Max Schmeling's manager) had a little trouble with good English (he's also famous for saying "We was robbed!"). He meant he should have *stayed* in bed. What a woman should do in bed, at least immediately after intercourse, is not only stay there, but take it a step further. Hoist your legs in the air and prop yourself up on your shoulders and elbows. Rest your legs against a wall or the bedpost, if the posts are high enough; the idea is to let gravity do its trick. Stay there for a long as you can without feeling completely ridiculous to your partner. Seriously. There is no harm in doing this, and it will help keep that precious swim team inside and on its way. This technique, passed down from the grandmother of a friend of my sister (see how important it is to talk to everybody . . .), was used long before test tubes were even a possibility. So if your doctor tells you to just go home and try it the way nature intended us to, try giving nature a little leg up, so to speak.

Let's call the whole thing off.

—Ira Gershwin,
song title

✳

Given the nature of your days, it's fair enough to cry "Uncle!" Being forced to do something day after day becomes initially boring, then annoying, then downright hateful. It's okay to drop the ball once in a while, to step back and take a break. Disengagement, even if briefly, can only help your state of mind. It's like fighting with your partner. There are times during a fight when it is all right, even wise, to call a halt to the name-calling and tension, and to ask that everyone take time out to cool down. When your schedule of conception becomes too much, as it surely does, then you should feel free to ask for a recess. And ask your partner to be understanding. She may wish for the same(!). If you take the lead, it may be a huge relief. The next time you are really fed up, call it off. It's only fair.

There is not a fiercer hell than the failure in a great object.

—*John Keats,*
preface to Endymion

*

You can't help but think the worst sometimes. Especially if you are facing a procedure like in-vitro fertilization, the odds in your favor are frighteningly low. What if you can never conceive? It's a bad place to let your mind wander, and when you do it will seem like there could be nothing worse, no fiercer hell. This is when it's important to keep in mind that in fact you haven't failed. You may be tired of trying—you even may be ready to give up. But don't. Miracles can happen.

I know of one couple who faced what were insurmountable obstacles. She had extensive scarring of her fallopian tubes; worse, she was over forty. The odds were horrible, but with the financial help of their parents, they were going to pursue in-vitro. The clinic was so busy they had to wait six months for the procedure. Then just before their appointment, he found out that he had antibodies in his semen that would make the in-vitro pointless. He would have to take antibiotics for a month, and the next available appointment was another six months away. After a few months passed they finally came to what they felt was their senses, and decided the in-vitro would be a waste of time and money. Knowing they could never conceive (she was told it was impossible), they pursued adoption instead. This also became a nightmare, but as it was their only option, they kept at it. In the meantime what couldn't happen happened. The doctors all said it was a medical impossibility, but she got pregnant anyway, and delivered a healthy baby. (True story.)

So don't feel like a failure yet. Miracles don't happen to everyone, but it could happen for you.

*

This very night I am going to leave off tobacco!

—Charles Lamb,
letter to Thomas Manning

✳

There's no getting around it. If you are serious about wanting to improve your chances of pregnancy, you will have to give up smoking. It is well known that nicotine decreases sperm count. Smoking is bad for your body; eventually, it will kill you. But before it does that, it dramatically reduces your chances for fatherhood. If you're a smoker, you smoke for all kinds of reasons, many of them understandable (to a smoker). But if you are serious about trying to up your fertility level, then the nicotine has to leave your body. Quit now, right now. As difficult as it will be—and, as a former two-pack-a-day man, I *know* how hard it will be—you must do it. Give your body a fighting chance. Plus, when you do become a parent, quitting now will increase your longevity, and therefore the time you have to spend with your child. Quit now.

Happy families are all alike; every unhappy family is unhappy in its own way.

—*Leo Tolstoy,*
Anna Karenina

It's true, nobody really knows your sorrow because every couple's battle with infertility is unique. It's helpful to hear the stories of others, of course, especially if their struggle was more difficult than yours is proving to be and was ultimately productive. But sometimes the last thing you want to hear or think about is someone else's story. Sometimes the stories don't make you feel better at all; sometimes they make you feel worse. It will never happen for me, you think. At such times you just need to muddle around in the sadness of your own story. Nobody but you knows how hard it is, how exhausting, how demoralizing. Yes, others have gone through the trials of in-vitro fertilization, but they couldn't possibly have faced the nightmare you do while trying to juggle the daily tests, the hormone shots, your job, your personal life. It's too damned hard to put a positive face on what you are doing all the time. So don't. It's okay to feel sorry for yourself.

*Nature is trying very hard to make us succeed,
but nature does not depend on us. We are not
the only experiment.*

—*R. Buckminster Fuller*

*

What the great architect and designer Fuller is saying,
in essence, is that the world is a much bigger place than
we can ever know, and that our role in it is, while significant to us, still infinitesimal. There are any number of
other lives and events happening, all as important to their
subjects as yours is to you. In the greater scheme of things,
you have to do the best you can by being the best kind of
person you can be. Your example of trust, love, and dedication might help someone else, in a way you may never
know about. You may be trying very hard to have a child,
and as yet the effort is not successful. But along the way
your actions may matter, and matter a lot, to those around
you. It's important that you remain optimistic and mind-
ful. This is not just about you.

Blessed are those that nought expect,
For they shall not be disappointed.

—John Wolcot,
"Ode to Pitt"

Yeh, right. How can you not expect success? Getting pregnant successfully is the whole point. But while it's impossible not to *want* success, it is possible not to *expect* it. You will save yourself a lot of grief if you can do this. You can't even be considered as "infertile" unless you've tried to conceive for a year without success; once you've entered the realm of assisted reproduction, the statistics, as you know, are not exactly encouraging. It's unusual, for instance, to conceive the first time you have an artificial insemination, and the average success rate for women under forty who undergo in-vitro fertilization is a little under one in five, and for GIFT (gamete intrafallopian transfer) a little over one in four. The statistics for women over forty are even worse. Even if your problem is a relatively simple one, like endometriosis, you will be more sane in the long run if you can suspend your expectations. It's a simple mind game, really, but if you don't expect to succeed, you will be a little less disappointed when your period rolls around, again. If your expectations are high (which *is* natural and understandable), your low when conception doesn't occur will be devastating. Playing this game doesn't mean you won't conceive, but it will help you through what can be a grueling process.

Nearly all men die of their remedies, and not of their illnesses.

—Molière,
The Imaginary Invalid

One of the most humiliating experiences a man can go through is that of being tested for infertility. Making the appointment, showing up on time, and talking to a nurse—usually female—about what needs to be done is laborious and annoying. Laborious, because it usually means taking time out from work to get to the medical office and to fill out the right papers. Annoying, because the procedure has an air of impersonality that is the very opposite of its (ultimate) human aim. And the actual production of a "sample" to be tested is appalling. You are handed a small plastic cup, and led into a closed room. Thoughtfully provided and pointed out by the nurse are stacks of ragged hard-core porn magazines. Sometimes, lucky you, a video is available as well. You put in your time, hand your cup to the nurse when you emerge, blush, and walk away as fast as possible.

If you don't have a sense of humor, you'll feel no small measure of shame and embarrassment. Take heart, though, and laugh about it. It's a necessary step on the path to what you really want. It's nasty, and feels ugly and sleazy, and is impersonal enough to turn you off to the actual act of love for a little while, if you let it. But remember how important it is to go through with what you're doing. You're half the process. So have a good laugh, and maybe even tell people you know (and trust) about it. Make a funny story out of it. This will help anyone else you know who also has to go through the same procedure. Don't let the weirdness of the occasion distance yourself from your ultimate goal.

Complacencies of the peignoir, and late
Coffee and oranges in a sunny chair.

—Wallace Stevens,
"Sunday Morning"

Most of us like our coffee in the morning. Some of us have a more serious relationship with it. Like all addictions, it's tough to give up, even if you only have one or two cups a day. I'll give it up when I get pregnant, you think, that's what's advised.

Give it up now. There are no conclusive studies on the effects of caffeine, but no expert is willing to say that it's good for you. Some studies have linked even moderate use to an increase in miscarriages, and it is likely that it affects fertility as well. Why fool around? Cut caffeine out of your daily diet no matter how much it means to you.

To be loved, be lovable.

—*Ovid,*
Amores

✳

Your spouse can't give you the love and affection you need if you don't let her. Sometimes you can get so twisted up in your own stuff that you appear hard and unreachable. Or, in response to a perceived coldness in your mate, you, in turn, grow hostile as well. Such maneuverings, natural as they are in the course of a relationship, lead nowhere that you want to be.

You need the love of each other now more than ever. No matter what lengths you may have to go to in order to conceive, you want the child to be born of love. Of course you can't always be loving and giving, but when you find yourself shutting down for too long, and perhaps even blaming your spouse for the distance between you, be honest with yourself. Are you being lovable? Don't you want to be loved?

A journey of a thousand miles must begin with a single step.

—Lao-tzu,
The Way of Lao-tzu

*

One of the biggest mistakes you can make is inaction. Many of us like to think that getting pregnant is supposed to be something that just happens. You decide you want to have a baby, you make love, you get pregnant. For an increasingly smaller number of people this is true. For you, it's different. You can apply Lao-tzu's wisdom to many things you might be dragging your feet about. Make the call to your friend's friend who thinks the world of the infertility expert she consulted. Start using an ovulation kit and take your temperature *every morning*. Doing so won't jinx conception. It will help you. It's a step. Get your husband to call the clinic that tests sperm and make an appointment today. Better yet, get him to stop putting off that call to the urologist. You put your feet in stirrups; the least he can do is bend over. There will be times when you think you can't do what you are supposed to do anymore. There will be times when the time for conception is right and the last thing you want to do is make love. Remember Lao-tzu. Take a single step.

I want to be alone.

—*Greta Garbo*

✳

Let's admit it: one of the difficult things about infertility, or about the "problem" of lack of conception, is that after a while you are crowded together with your partner too much of the time. Doctors' appointments, counseling sessions, medical discussions, informational readings, conversations with other people—everything is done together, all the time. There's no opportunity, it seems, for any time for and by yourself. Just time to read, or think, or space out if you want. That time is really important. You need to take time off, on a regular basis, to keep your head clear. Otherwise, you'll start to feel so crowded you'll lose it. And everything will spin out of whack. It's perfectly acceptable to step back and ask for a period of nonengagement. The incessant white noise of a busy schedule together isn't healthy in the long run. Don't worry about being tagged unsociable, or unfriendly. Your partner will —*must*—understand. She needs it too, as much as you do.

People often grudge others what they cannot enjoy themselves.

—Aesop,
"The Dog in the Manger"

*

One of the more upsetting side effects of not getting pregnant is how much you resent those who are. Complete strangers manage to tear your heart out. Walking down crowded streets or through malls is unbearable—all you see are pregnant women, or pregnant women with young children hanging onto them. Some stores even have parking spaces for pregnant women! Worse, some clinics and hospitals make pregnant and infertile women alike share the same waiting rooms or wards! The whole world seems to be pregnant except you, as though you are the victim of a cruel conspiracy. The last thing you are able to feel is joy for anyone who has achieved what you haven't yet. It's a horrible state of mind, but totally normal. Just try and look the other way. It's all you can do.

In both men and women, even moderate drinking can . . . cause at least a temporary bout with infertility.

—*infertility newsgroup advice posted on the Internet*

Like smoking, drinking alcohol is the very last thing someone battling with infertility should be doing to their body. Alcohol is pure poison; delicious, and with a fun effect, but straight poison nonetheless. The doctor will tell you that, as a basic, you should avoid all alcohol in any form *at least* forty-eight hours before attempting to conceive. It can get very hard to track a restriction such as this, especially when, hopefully, you will work yourself into the mood to try to conceive at any time. If you haven't been careful for the preceding forty-eight hours, your chances of success are far, far fewer. Why not give yourself the best possible chance at what you want so very much? Stop drinking for a while. No wine, no cocktails, not even a beer. Your chances will increase remarkably, the medical profession believes. And why not try it? What do you have to lose? (And won't it be a pleasure to wake up refreshed, instead of bleary?)

Hope springs eternal in the human breast:
Man never is, but always to be blest.

—*Alexander Pope,*
An Essay on Man

Hope is your salvation. You constantly face a multitude of demons—the grueling tests, many of which are daily; the escalating financial costs; your biological clock which seems to tick louder with each passing month. It's enough to bury you with despair, yet you persevere. You continue to hope for the best, and so you should. Hope gets you up in the morning and lets you perform at night. It allows you to rise above the daunting statistics and probability rates and triumph over the humorless experts who cower in fear of malpractice suits. It ensures that you keep your perspective, and it keeps you from going crazy. Without hope you would be lost in the maze of modern technology.

The most beautiful thing we can experience is the mysterious.

—*Albert Einstein,*
What I Believe

*

As children of a scientific age, in which there seem to be few if any mysteries left, we expect to be told the whys about everything. In the days of our grandparents, world maps had more than one blank space, white-colored territory that was unknown to and uncharted by Western civilization. Today we know every inch of the planet (which is not to the planet's benefit).

Similarly, we want to be told about every inch of humanity, both physical and psychic. It is thought unacceptable to have white spaces in our outlines of ourselves. But so much of life can't be explained rationally. There are vast tracts of mystery left to the human map, and that is as it should be.

Birth is truly a miracle. That it happens, or doesn't, is part of that blank space too, and that is as it should be.

Too much investigation and interference can be a Pandora's box. Leave some mystery in your life. It does have a purpose, perhaps greater than human understanding.

★

Shall we make a new rule of life from tonight: always to try to be a little kinder than is necessary?

—*Sir J. M. Barrie,*
The Little White Bird

A little extra kindness with each other will go a long way toward smoothing out the tensions that inevitably exist between the two of you. This holds true for any married couple, for that matter, but is perhaps especially true for couples facing the stresses of infertility. It may be that you are simply tired of being there for each other, or that you are tired of constantly being the one to direct your efforts. It may be that only one of you is unable to conceive and the burden is sometimes too great. It may be merely that your boss yelled at you and was justified in doing so. If you haven't already, make it a new house rule. Be a little kinder, even if you don't feel like it.

A friend may well be reckoned the masterpiece of Nature.

> —*Ralph Waldo Emerson,*
> *Essays*

*

It is time now to set aside your worries about having children. Stop wrestling with your partner about The Issue. Make the day be for someone else. Pick up the phone and call someone you like. Make a lunch date with him or her. Wander into their office for a chat, stop by their house after work, write—and send—a letter. Whatever you do, make it revolve, for a little while, around a person you have been friends with. Don't bring up the subject of kids, at least not your own desire for kids. Keep your worries out of it. Take the time to talk about whatever is on your friend's mind. In short, cultivate another subject besides your own worry. The friends you make and have kept are a very important part of your life. It can be easy to neglect them, especially when you are fixated on a big problem. Don't. Your friends matter even more than you might think. To be able to make a friend, and keep one, is a kind of lifeline. As the years pass, that lifeline grows stronger. The associations you share together, and the memories, add up to a valuable element of your emotional makeup. Get in touch with one friend or another now. It's important.

The great decisions of human life have as a rule far more to do with the instincts and other mysterious unconscious factors than with conscious will and well-meaning reasonableness.

—Carl Jung,
Modern Man in Search of a Soul

✳

Everybody wants to trust their intuition, and hardly anybody does. But if you want to control your situation as much as possible, you will need to start listening to that inner voice. The one that nags at you because you think maybe you should be seeing a specialist, even though your trusted and familiar OB/GYN claims to be able to do a lot of the tests. (See a specialist.) Or worse, your OB has you on Clomid without putting you through *any* of the tests. (Go off Clomid and see a specialist.) Sometimes your specialist will recommend procedures that you sense aren't working—one couple felt it was time to move on to IVF (in-vitro fertilization) and their doctor wanted to stick with more IUIs (intrauterine insemination). While the results aren't in on this particular case, I think it's important to trust your gut, if only to allow yourself to have some control.

"Protocols" be damned. One doctor allowed herself to follow her instincts regarding hormone dosages, despite the program protocol, and her IVF patient's uterine lining was *much* better than before. Such intelligence, based on instinct, may mean all the difference. What do you have to lose?

Henceforth, I ask not good fortune, I myself am good fortune.

—*Walt Whitman,*
"Song of the Open Road"

What the great poet Walt Whitman meant was this: don't look elsewhere for your identity, or for your source of happiness, or for something good to take place. *You* are the good news. You have the ability to be what you want: happy, healthy, sane. It is tempting to rely on others all the time, for the things that make you feel happy. That puts you in a dangerous position. If something doesn't come through, then you turn around and blame someone else. Things will take a definite turn for the better when you realize that, in fact, you create your own reality, and that the best source of happiness lies within your own soul. To maximize this feeling may take a long time. It may take a period of retreat from regular sources of anxiety. It may take changing ways you've gotten very accustomed to. But once it is done, the feeling of freedom you then experience will be like a rush of fresh air. Your being is your own good fortune. It's up to you to believe this, and to use this knowledge wisely.

As long as you know that most men are like children you know everything.

—Coco Chanel

*

In the sense that they need to have their hands held, this is indeed true. Many people facing infertility, especially in the early stages, have to deal with reluctant spouses. Almost as if they are three-year-olds being asked to get dressed, they simply will not, cannot, participate willingly in the process when it involves them directly. Semen samples? Forget it. Visit the urologist or proctologist? Even worse. Questioning the purpose of many tests? All the time. "Do I have to?" is a line familiar to many of us. So take your spouse by the hand, encourage him, praise him, then yell at him if you have to. Do whatever it takes. Think of it as practice for the children that are to come.

Truth has no special time of its own. Its hour is now—always.

—Albert Schweitzer,
Out of My Life and Thought

If you are feeling down about the whole thing, admit it. Then tell your partner. Include her in what you're feeling. Let the healing begin by being honest with yourselves. As long as you deny your sadness, your anxiety, your self-doubt, you'll be mired in trouble up to your ears. Let yourself start to go free by sharing your fears. The truth can only help.

Being honest about any depression you feel may completely surprise your partner, especially if you tend to keep your feelings concealed or like to be stoic. And it may be the trigger that releases a flow of conversation with real depth about the issues you are both facing. If you are known to be reserved, try letting it out. You'll feel much better, and you'll let fresh air into your relationship.

Ye have heard of the patience of Job.

—James 5:11

✳

For most couples facing problems conceiving, patience is a tough lesson to learn. Like Job, it seems as though we must endure endless suffering; unlike Job, most of us, especially as time wears on, are not so sure of our faith—in God, in medicine, in ourselves. Keep in mind, though, that as difficult as conception might be for you, you too can be patient.

Even if your religious background is less than solid, it might help you to pray and to contemplate the purpose of your suffering—or, if it's easier, contemplate the story of Job. A wealthy and prosperous man, he lost everything and suffered terribly. As his troubles increased, his friends constantly questioned the wisdom of his faith. But he hung in there, and ultimately his suffering and his faith were rewarded by his merciful God. He died old and happy, living long enough to see his great-grandchildren. Yes, we have all heard of the patience of Job, even if we haven't known what that literally means. It might help to apply the lesson of his story to your own suffering.

I would like a simple life
yet all night I am laying
poems away in a long box.

—Anne Sexton,
"The Ambition Bird"

★

All you want is to be happy. It isn't asking much. If only you had a child. If only you were a *family*. Everything would fall into place and you'd feel much better about the way your life is going. Right?

Actually, your life is going pretty well. You are in a loving relationship. Your health and well-being, your aspirations, your *self*, matter deeply to your partner. As hers matters equally to you. Together, you are both making a life and are growing together, experiencing the heady joys of partnership and adulthood.

You will be a parent eventually, a fine one who enjoys the role of mentor, protector, guide. For now, though, take a moment to stop and enjoy your life. Stop projecting so much. Give time to the immediate moment. Don't agonize over the might-have-beens. The here and now is too important. Live in the present.

Abortions will not let you forget.
You remember the children you got that
you did not get.

—Gwendolyn Brooks,
"The Mother,"
A Street in Brownsville

Abortion is a tricky issue, which is why it is important
to address it here. Those of us who have had abortions
face an extra hell when confronting infertility. Things that
you do in your youth rarely come back to haunt you the
way abortion does. The knowledge that you were once
able to create life when you weren't able to handle it, and
now are unable to create a life when you *are* able to handle
it is hard to reconcile. It must be a just punishment, you
think, even if ordinarily you wouldn't condemn abortion
on moral grounds. What if that mistake in college was my
only chance, you wonder, as though children are meted
out by predestined lottery.

While you will have to find your own way around this
issue, don't just bury it. Painful as it is to look back, it is
worth reviewing the reasons for a previous abortion to
avoid the extra level of purgatory that comes from regret-

ting one. There is not, as you might let yourself think, an allotment of chances to get pregnant that you used up before you were ready. Nor is your current inability to conceive a delayed punishment from a higher being. It's something you did a long time ago, and just as you moved on from it then, you need to move on from it now.

The best part of married life is the fights. The rest is merely so-so.

—*Thornton Wilder,*
The Matchmaker

*

All right, give in to it. The whole situation makes you furious. You're angry about the issue of childbearing, you're angry nothing seems to be happening, you're angry at your mate for being awful, for nagging, for the endless questioning. Fair enough. So let fly. Pick a fight. Say what you think. To keep a relationship healthy and fresh, sometimes you have to let your darker feelings out in the open. Suppressing your anger, repressing your jags of temper, won't help. They'll do the opposite—make you madder, more resentful, more hostile. And hostility isn't something you need at this point in your life. So let it out. Your mate will react with equal anger, perhaps, and if you both can get angry without going too far overboard, the festering will be lanced. Really. (You can test it out in a mild way first.) A good fair fight will clear the air, your mind, and your heart. Just don't get into it too much.

Slow and steady wins the race.

—Aesop,
"The Hare and the Tortoise"

Sayings like this can make you tired before you even begin. Trying to have a baby shouldn't be such hard work. It should be easy, natural.

Beware the arrogance of the hare. You might want to believe that you will be divinely blessed by conception, but more often than not, it works the other way. Think about it. There is a tiny window of opportunity in which to conceive—three days at most out of the month. The more you put your mind to it, the greater your chances for success. Even if you think you have a grasp on the days when you can get pregnant, you probably don't. I consider myself fairly good at understanding basic biology, but nevertheless, it took me at least a year before I finally understood the full importance of taking your basal temperature every morning. Many women don't want to bother with this, preferring ovulation kits instead. These are vital too, but start with a thermometer. After six months you'll begin to see a surprising pattern and after a year you can see just where your body temperature drops as you are about to release an egg. No matter what other obstacles might stand in your way, this information will help you win the race, slow and steady, every morning.

A bore is a man who, when you ask him how he is, tells you.

—Bert Taylor,
The So-Called Human Race

*

You know the questions all too well: "Do you have any kids?"; "Aren't you planning to have any?"; "What are you waiting for?"; "What's the problem?" People can be thoughtless in their comments. As tempting as it may be to throw back a tart rejoinder ("We're waiting for you to die so we can inherit your money and then have the kind of life we *really* want"), don't be thoughtless in your response. It would be too easy to lose it and talk back angrily, or with sadness. In fact, few people really need to know what you are going through. Save your heartfelt answers for those friends who truly care. You'll know who they are. Respond to the thoughtless questions gently, saying something like, "If we're lucky, we'll have children soon" or "No problem—it will happen when the time is right" or "Life is pretty good right now. Isn't it for you?" The talks you have with the right people will make a big difference to how you look at things, and will be a sure comfort. Talking about your feelings with just anyone won't necessarily help you or them. And saving your emotional energy for the people who matter can help in a hundred different ways.

Who shall decide when doctors disagree?

—Alexander Pope,
"To Lord Bathurst,"
Moral Essays

You shall. Don't make the mistake of putting yourself entirely in your doctor's hands. You may or may not have one or more doctors advising you, but make sure you are the one driving the bus. Your doctors are invaluable, of course, but they are not infallible, nor do they know or are they able to explain *everything*. There are many books on the subject of infertility, and while you shouldn't bother to read every one, it's more than a good idea to at least be aware of what's out there. It is also wise to at least consider alternative therapies. Your doctor may not know or may not appreciate the benefits of herbs or acupuncture, for example. Acupuncture is more commonly sought by patients experiencing physical pain, but any female of childbearing age who has tried acupuncture knows that the treatments can make you more fertile. Seeing an acupuncturist won't necessarily make you conceive, but it does make the circulation of fluids in your body move more freely by helping to restore balance to your system. It can also be an effective stress reducer, as can yoga and meditation. If you weren't suffering from stress before, you will be after numerous trips to doctors' offices. Follow their advice, but follow your own as well.

Dreams are necessary to life.

—Anaïs Nin,
The Diary of Anaïs Nin

Let yourself daydream about it. Flood your mind with the images of parenting, of little children. Revel in the joy you will feel, and feel the joy even as you do so. The happiness that a positive daydream about a cherished hope can bring will astound you. Even if it's only for a few minutes, that dream will help direct your energies and will refocus your thoughts. Giving in to wishful thinking, if it's happy and not regretful, can motivate you and make you feel happy about what you want. It's a feeling that is all too easy to lose in the rush of other emotions. Nothing is more energizing, in the long run, than positive parenting. Your daydreams can help you get there.

While it is a time of great tragedy, nothing is being lost but money.

—John Kenneth Galbraith,
The Great Crash, 1929

Money is a tricky subject. Galbraith was referring to the panic that led to the greatest financial disaster of all time, but his words can apply to your world as well. The money necessary to combat even the simplest cases of infertility can pose a strain on your resources, to say the least. Ovulation kits are a mere $30, but it adds up as the months tick by. So do the diagnostic tests and the specialists. And then there's the equivalent of the 1929 crash, high-tech assisted reproduction, with per-cycle costs ranging from an average of $300 for IUI to $10,000 for IVF, and even more for the relatively new ICSI (intracytoplasmic sperm injection). The fertility drugs alone cost at least $2,000 a pop. To make matters worse, the health insurance available to most people covers only a fraction of the total.

It's grim. And the weight of it does make your own

personal tragedy that much more complicated. But it is only money. Each of us has to determine what our limits are, how much we can afford, how much we can beg and borrow. There is nothing wrong with waiting until you can afford to see specialists, just as there is nothing wrong with spending your entire savings on IVF. In the meantime, maybe our health-insurance industry will follow the lead of European countries whose health plans generally pay for at least four or five tries.

The first and great commandment is, Don't let them scare you.

—Elmer Davis,
But We Were Born Free

✳

After many months getting nowhere in our efforts to have a child, there were times when the bad news added up to a very real sense of fear that went beyond mere (and familiar) anxiety. We would both lie awake, worried sick and unable to voice our worries aloud to each other. The fear took in a lot of individual items: Would we *never* have children? Was something wrong, physically, not just about fertility, but something deeper and darker? Were we right for each other as a couple? Could we survive this and still feel good about each other? Had we each made a terrible mistake?

The fear itself is scary, as Franklin Roosevelt famously noted when he took office during the Depression. And if you let it, it can envelop you in a miasma that will threaten other parts of your daily life. Don't let it do so. Don't give in to it. And don't believe it. Fear is as powerful as you allow it to be. Don't start questioning your partner. Ride with it, if you can. Your challenge is to stay calm and even-keeled. Recognize the dark side of what you're going through, but bypass its seduction. That way leads only to serious trouble. Keep your mind clear. You have much, much more important things to focus on than your anxiety.

The midnight train is whining low,
I'm so lonesome, I could cry.

—Hank Williams,
"I'm So Lonesome I Could Cry"

Infertility is a lonely place. It consumes your waking thoughts and colors almost every emotion. No matter how close you are to your friends, there comes a point at which you can't confide in them anymore. You feel as though either your despair is too much a burden for them, or, even worse, that if you articulate the depth of your heartache, the reality will overwhelm you. And even though your spouse knows exactly how you are feeling, or at least can empathize, you feel you can't burden him either: he has his own stuff to deal with.

All of the above is true. But when you start to drown in your sorrow, make yourself reach out. Let yourself have a good cry now and then—or often if you need to. But remember that you are not alone. Your friends want to be there for you if you'd just let them. More important, your spouse is probably lying there in the dark feeling the same way. Comfort each other, you'll feel better.

I see London, I see France,
I see someone's underpants.

—children's rhyme

It sounds silly at first, but the type of underwear you prefer can be of vital importance. If you haven't heard it already, pay attention here. You should be wearing boxer shorts whether you (or your mate) like them or not. One of the simplest things you can do to maximize good sperm production is let the family jewels dangle. Sperm are best manufactured and matured at a certain temperature (below ninety-five degrees). There is a reason why the scrotum hangs outside the body—it's too hot inside. So be sure to wear loose-fitting shorts, and loose blue jeans, too, for that matter.

*Where is the wisdom we have lost in
    knowledge?*
*Where is the knowledge we have lost in
    information?*

—*T. S. Eliot,*
The Rock

There will be times when the science of infertility experts threatens to overwhelm you. Conception, in essence, is nothing short of a miracle. The science of conception, however, goes against the grain of everything you might like to believe in. The tests, the clinics, even the doctors who are leading you through the maze of possibilities and procedures, can be heartless, cold, businesslike. Infertility treatments are, in fact, a business, which is why it is important for you to sort out how you feel about the process. I felt the medical technology available to us was, like conception itself, nothing short of a miracle. And feeling this way allowed me to find a quiet, spiritual place within myself that helped me deal with the procedures recommended to us (in our case, sperm washing and artificial insemination). My husband, by contrast, was paralyzed by the prospect of playing God. He couldn't see the wisdom of our approach and instead was overwhelmed and dismayed by the technical information. On the eve of our scheduled insemination, he announced he wasn't sure we should go through with it. "Maybe it's not meant to be," he said. I pointed out that if it wasn't meant to be, we wouldn't have access to such medical technology. A hundred years ago, we simply would have been "barren." He was able to come around to my way of thinking, and the following morning we were able to both laugh at the absurdity of the procedure, and cry at the possible success of it.

Fear tastes like a rusty knife and do not let her into your house.

—*John Cheever,*
The Wapshot Chronicle

✳

That you are having difficulty getting pregnant may be due to medical causes. Often, men will experience a condition called *varioceles*. This is when dilated veins in the genitals increase the temperature of the scrotum, and usually result in a much lower sperm count or in malfunctioning sperm. If this is the case, surgery—a procedure called *variocelectomy*—is the solution. It is relatively simple, and it will do the trick if indeed varioceles is the problem.

In my opinion there is little more frightening than surgery of any kind. Even basic dental work—teeth cleaning, for instance—terrifies me. The idea of a doctor approaching my private parts with a knife is enough to make me move far, far away into the woods. If you are facing this kind of surgery, I have no doubt you are afraid. Try to focus, if you can, on the end result. Any kind of surgery is nervous-making and prone to morbid fantasies. But variocelectomy is straightforward, standard, and frequently done. Men who go through it report their efforts at pregnancy greatly enhanced, and often successful. It's worth going through it, to better your chances for conceiving. You may have been through an appendectomy, or a kidney stone, or hemorrhoidal surgery, or some other relatively minor work. This will be the same thing. Really.

Fear will tell you to avoid what you need to do. Don't give in to it. It will take courage on your part, but know that the procedure is relatively common, the actual surgery is not dangerous, and the result could lead to what you want so very much.

> *'Tis the part of a wise man to keep himself to-day for tomorrow, and not venture all his eggs in one basket.*
>
> —*Miguel de Cervantes,*
> *Don Quixote de la Mancha*

Cervantes's wisdom has become somewhat of a cliché in today's culture, and a bitter pill for any woman facing infertility. It is a cruel twist of evolutionary fate that in fact, literally, all our eggs *are* in one basket. As most women know, we are born with the eggs we will later conceive with; the older we are, the older our eggs are. The older the eggs, the more difficult it is to conceive, or the riskier it is, or both. The statistics are worth ignoring, however. You should acquaint yourself with them, of course; it would be foolish not to, but especially if you are over forty, you should focus on the stories of women who managed to triumph over the statistics. A woman with severe endometriosis who conceived after eight years. The woman who tried for *ten years,* got pregnant through in-vitro after transferring just *one* embryo, and gave birth to a healthy baby girl.

Such stories point to something else. Cervantes's words were metaphorical, obviously, and thus can be heeded and can be comforting. You must always keep a part of yourself prepared for the possibilities of tomorrow, for what may be devastating failure today, in the next cycle may be the news that you've worked so hard for. Technically all your eggs are in one basket, but each month you get to try again.

The reward of labor is life.

—*William Morris,*
News From Nowhere

✳

You know that feeling all too well. It's the right time for conception, but you just aren't in the mood. You've had a fight and can't stand to look at each other. You're tired. Fair enough. If you can't, you can't. But if, maybe, you can turn that feeling of anger into one of love, if you can drop your grudge, forgive, set things aside—are the problems really that serious?—then the miracle might happen. It's certainly worth trying. Although it might seem to you that nothing would be worth it, the possibility of new life *is*. And even if nothing happens but a hug and a smile, that's worth it too. There's enough anger in the world without keeping your own little flame going, to no ultimate good. Kiss and make up, and see what happens. It just might mean life.

The poetry of earth is never dead.

—*John Keats*,
"*On the Grasshopper and the Cricket*"

✳

When you are feeling particularly miserable and depressed, sometimes the best cure is to venture outside and try to find solace in nature. If you live in a city, take long and frequent walks in a park or, even better, a public garden. Over time you will notice both the subtle and dramatic changes that occur throughout the seasons. If you have your own garden, spend time each day, if you can, working the earth, planting seeds and young plants, dividing perennials to expand your garden or give to friends. Simply weeding or inspecting your garden's progress can do wonders for a wounded psyche. By creating and nurturing plant life you can be encouraged about your own.

Stress may adversely affect sperm production.
—medical study

*

A common source of debate among medical researchers is whether stress, which is known to be physically harmful and even fatal to some people, has an equally negative effect on sperm production and fertility. Some say, when alcohol is invoked as a fertility inhibitor, that previous generations drank and smoked like crazy and had no problem conceiving. That may be true—although we have no way of knowing how many problem pregnancies and births there were before modern medicine started tracking these things. But there can be little doubt, in a commonsense approach, that stress will hurt your chances of getting pregnant. Anxiety, fear, anger; inability to achieve arousal; sparring with your partner as a way to deal with hostility and stress and thus avoid intimacy; these all must hurt conception. While the medical evidence is still sketchy, realize that, like anything else that doesn't make you feel good, stress is something you want to avoid. Meditate, go on a walk, try to clear your mind—there are a hundred ways to combat stress. But clear it away you must. Otherwise, you are really hurting yourself.

*It's all right for a woman to be, above all,
human. I am a woman first of all.*

—*Anaïs Nin,*
The Diary of Anaïs Nin

It's easy to feel a sense of failure as a woman when
your body has failed you in terms of reproduction. It's
normal to feel this way—it's human. Just because you
haven't gotten pregnant the first time out, and even if you
are still not pregnant after two or four or even eight years
of trying, you are still a woman, and you are only human.
Sometimes the process you are going through seems in-
human, but whether you know it or not, the day-to-day
challenges you face are making you a stronger, more
deeply realized person. The courage it takes to confront
the dismal realities of infertility, the *humility* required to
meet the failures and obstacles, are making you more
human.

So keep perspective on your role as a woman. Don't
forget or ignore those aspects of yourself that contribute
to who you are. If you are to successfully go through the

trials of infertility, you need to maintain a strong sense of self. Remind yourself that you are only human and that you are still valid as a woman, even though you are having trouble conceiving. Gain strength from what you are facing, but don't feel you have to be superhuman in order to get through it.

How many cares one loses when one decides not to be something but to be someone.

—Coco Chanel

✳

For many, many months now, or even longer, you have been trying to conceive. Increasingly, your view of yourself, as a person and as a couple, has been changing. From two people who love each other and want children, you are heading into the dreaded void of "childless couple" or "infertile couple." Or worse, you may start to be referred to as "poor" so-and-so. This is because you have made such a drama with your friends and colleagues about your desire to conceive. It has become your prime topic of conversation, the focus of your daily life. As such, other people have learned to treat your sorrow with the importance you yourself have given it. But you need to break out of this trap. Because, in reality, you are more than just "poor" whomever. You have a full life, a partner who loves you, an entire existence. Live your life. Be a rounded person. Talk about other things besides your problems.

There's nothing wrong with including people you care about in your tribulations, but unless you want to box yourself into an unpleasant emotional identity, try to break out and explore other sides to your life. You'll be surprised by the range you may find there.

Hurry up please its time.

—*T. S. Eliot,*
"The Game of Chess,"
The Waste Land

Nothing will put more of a damper on your sex life than command performances. Unfortunately, for couples trying to get pregnant, command performances are about all you have to look forward to. When your basal temperature and your ovulation tester say it's time, it's time. And then, whether you want to or not, you get to do it for three or four days straight, or three or four alternating days, at which point you feel like you never want to have sex again. Even if you do want to, the specter of carelessly using up quantities of sperm when they won't be productive can be a damper as well. Essentially you're limited to less than one week out of four and then you have to perform, in a sense, against the clock. For obvious reasons, this is more difficult for the male, but it's not easy for either of you. All I can say is try to keep your eyes on the prize. I know of one man who had to leave the room and pray. Lucky for him, it worked.

Outside the open window
The morning air is all awash with angels.

—*Richard Wilbur,*
"*Love Calls Us to the Things of This World*"

*

Any morning at all is a good time to start afresh. If you had a fight with your partner, and the hard and hurtful words are still stinging, patch it up right now. It doesn't matter who was right, who was wrong. Clear the air.

If you've been feeling trapped in some idea that has been generating intense negativity, throw the window open (figuratively) and let in some fresh air and new possibilities. Turn over a new leaf, whatever the issue may be. The air around you *is* awash with angels, or hopes, or good things. Open yourself up to the magic of the day.

Women are wiser than men because they know less and understand more.

—James Stephens,
The Crock of Gold

We often know more, too. At least when it comes to the basics of reproduction, most women know the practical information much better than men—after all, we've been controlling conception with various methods for many years. By extention, it is easier for us to understand the highly technical information inherent in assisted reproduction as well. And does this make us wiser? I think it helps us accept the realities, whatever they are, and to hang in there whatever the costs. It's harder for those men who feel that they can show up and do what's asked of them, but who don't really understand, or take the time to make themselves understand, especially in technical terms, what's happening.

So if this is your situation, make the effort to help your spouse. Even if it seems as though he's not really interested or is even paying attention, he should know what you know. Don't assume that he does. You've been counting the days since the onset of your last period, but he might have lost track. He might not fully appreciate the wisdom of holding off on sex (and letting his semen build up) just before ovulation time, but you can help him to understand why.

*

In America there are two classes of travel—first class, and with children.

—Robert Benchley,
"Kiddie-Kar Travel"

There are times when you need to revel in the lack of children in your life. This is not meant as a cruel comment. But really, enjoy your freedom of movement. One day, with luck, you will have a child. For now, though, think of what is open to you that is not open to parents on a regular basis: You can, on the spur of the moment, go out for dinner. You can see a movie without worrying about getting a baby-sitter. You can go out for a walk, take a nap, drop in on a friend. You can come home late from work. Of course, none of these diversions really matter, especially if you feel the lack of children as deeply as you surely do. But, for a few hours, it is worth remembering that you still have unparalleled freedom to move at will. It is a luxury parents envy as much as you envy their role as parents. The option to simply disappear for a few hours is rare. Enjoy the time. Use it with style. Or even use it to do nothing at all. Once children arrive, the opportunity to be your own master, time-wise, will disappear for years to come. Few parents-to-be truly understand this. Even fewer take advantage of it before it is too late. So, as flippant as it sounds, it is meant sincerely. *Take the time.* You won't be sorry.

Yet we have gone on living,
Living and partly living.

—*T. S. Eliot,*
Murder in the Cathedral

When you are so obsessed with a single, seemingly unattainable goal, one which has the power to transform your life, it is hard to go on living, day after day, as though your life is normal. Yet you do. Or you try to. The little deaths of disappointment you experience are to be expected, however, and if you feel as though you are just moving through your existence, half there, partly alive, know that this, too, will pass.

*It's difficult for a discontented man not to re-
proach someone else, whoever is closest to him,
for his own discontent.*

—Leo Tolstoy,
Anna Karenina

The obvious thing is to blame your partner for what
you are both going through right now. Lack of fertility
can't be your fault. Or if it is (and if you think of it as a
"fault") your partner is making it all worse by bad behavior, bad temper, bad personality generally. Doesn't that
conviction make you feel better? And doesn't taking out
your anger on your partner make you just a tiny bit
happier?

Get over it, and fast. Blaming your partner in *any* way
is destructive if you keep it up. Putting up a dividing line
between the two of you, building a wall to separate your
lives emotionally, will make you momentarily happy. But
you'll soon be more misreable than before, when the sense
of aloneness sinks in. Try not to hurt your partner like
this. Blame, while easy to do, has never been productive.
Work together to come together as friends and life
partners.

All I really really want our love to do
is to bring out the best in me and you too.

—Joni Mitchell,
"All I Want"

As with overcoming any adversity, battling infertility will at times bring out the worst and the best in you. Trying to get pregnant can be so much work you can forget to take the time to have fun. The relationship you have with your spouse is of primary importance—you may or may not conceive, but you will always have each other. Take advantage of it. Don't give in to loneliness or worse, hurting each other. Go dancing, go to a dive bar and play all your favorite songs on the jukebox, splurge on a fancy candlelit dinner, plan a vacation to a spot you've always talked about visiting and make the time to actually go there. Working to get pregnant can make you feel tired and old, so come on, belong to the living.

Goodness had nothing to do with it.

—Mae West

*

Now that your love life has been scheduled, programmed, timed, and processed to death, wouldn't you rather be living on a desert island? Alone? Probably you would. If so, it's time to rekindle the sense of desire for your partner that has been such an important part of your life together. Remember the excitement you felt when making love? It's there, and won't ever really go away. It's just been buried by the relentless nature of what you have been going through. Put aside, for a little while, your anxieties about infertility. Just for a little while. Think about your partner, try to feel that side of your love life that isn't wired to a timer. Be bad with her. Think downright dirty thoughts, and act them out. If you can get to a place where you have both been together, *before* all the trials of conception, then, for at least this one encounter, you will remember why you are together and what fire there really is in your life together.

In the deepest heart of all of us there is a corner in which the ultimate mystery of things works sadly.

—William James,
The Will to Believe

✳

The mystery inherent in unexplained infertility makes it perhaps the hardest type of infertility to bear. The doctors tell you that physically, nothing is wrong. You think you should feel relieved, maybe even lucky, and for a time you do. But if months and then years roll by, the lack of a specific problem looms like a dark, mysterious cloud. Without knowing what to treat, how do you treat it? There is an odd power that comes from battling an identifiable foe—whether it be low sperm count, blocked tubes, polycystic ovaries, endometriosis, all of the above —and a great sadness that comes from fighting something that technically doesn't exist. *Something* must be wrong, you think, something *has* to be. After three, four, five years, it can't simply be that you and your spouse just need to relax. (And woe to the person who tells you to do so.)

You need to remember that unexplained infertility, like

other kinds of infertility, is treatable. It's just that you have to play more of a Russian roulette with the treatments available to couples with specific problems. Maybe GIFT will work for you as it has for others in your situation; maybe Clomid will do the trick. And the psychological strategy is the same as it is for couples with severe physical hurdles to circumvent: Don't let the sadness overwhelm you; take control by taking it one month at a time.

In a real dark night of the soul it is always three o'clock in the morning.

—F. Scott Fitzgerald,
The Crack-Up

*

Fitzgerald himself was no stranger to depression, famously and tragically. That feeling, the black dog that chews at your heart, may be the most dangerous thing to beset you—except for lack of trust in your partner. No doubt you know many people who are paralyzed by depression, who feel trapped, who can't see a way out. At all costs, don't allow depression to take over your head. Once it gets a foothold, you're (temporarily) sunk. Distract yourself with things or people, do whatever it takes. Just don't get pulled into the darkness. It's easy to allow yourself to feel bad. In a strange sort of way, it can even be comforting. Banish it! The comfort of it is, in fact, a ruse, and can only prove harmful.

*Well, we all need someone we can lean on,
And if you want it, well, you can lean on me.*

—*Mick Jagger and Keith Richards,*
"Let It Bleed"

*

Your family and friends are there, *waiting* for you to lean on them. Infertility is not a subject you can initiate, unless you are the person experiencing it. But your friends want to help you if they can, whether it's just listening to your latest sadness, or taking you out on the town to get your mind off things.

Sometimes, for no good reason, we are afraid to reach out and ask for help. But when you do, you'll feel so much better. There will be times when you'll feel like a repetitive burden to your friends, always calling up with the same refrain about how sad you are, or afraid. And yet when you do lean on them, you are able to quickly move on. And they are grateful they are able to be there for you.

Another option is to join or just listen in to the infertility newsgroup on the Internet. "Alt.infertility" provides scores of postings on just about every aspect of infertility and if you simply want to "vent" your feelings, there is always a comforting response from someone who knows exactly how you feel.

What we've got here is a failure to communicate.

—Donn Pearce,
Cool Hand Luke

★

Your partner is the most important person in your life, bar none. It is essential, for your marriage or partnership to work at all, that you have complete trust in each other. While this is often taken to mean sexual fidelity, it is as important to preserve emotional trust. Your sexual relationship is, obviously, tremendously important. But you have to be able to speak openly with each other. You have to be able to share your fears and hopes, and exchange feelings, without worrying that your partner will think badly of you, or won't take you seriously. Communication is of paramount importance—there is nothing more important in your relationship. Talk to each other; confide; ask questions. Don't be afraid of saying what's on your mind, even if it sounds ridiculous. It isn't.

Love seeketh not itself to please,
Nor for itself hath any care,
But for another gives its ease,
And builds a Heaven in Hell's despair.

—*William Blake,*
"The Clod and the Pebble"

✳

Take comfort in each other. For those times when you find yourself sinking into the depths of despair, remember that your spouse is there for you, the person who knows you best and still loves you at your worst. Chances are, if you are feeling truly terrible, he might be less so—or at least able to set his anguish aside to ease yours. I remember once asking my husband to simply hold me. I didn't even know how sad I was until I felt his arms around me and then there was no stopping my tears, great wrenching sobs from months of not really letting go. When I was finally spent, I thanked him, and he seemed so surprised. I love you, he said, this is what I'm here for.

Pessimism, when you get used to it, is just as agreeable as optimism.

—Arnold Bennett,
Things That Have Interested Me

*

Don't you often find that crankiness can feel good? That being angry can really be satisfying? That looking on the dark side seems just right?

We're always told to believe in the power of positive thinking. Optimism will supposedly improve one's health and generally promote one's well-being. And that may well be true. But there are times when a perky smile isn't enough. If you are going through hard times, sometimes allowing yourself to feel down, angry, or depressed will help you feel better. You *are* feeling like nothing ever goes right or will ever go right. So why not give in to it, and wallow a little? It's an accurate reflection of your current state of emotions. And repressing what you're feeling all the time can prove harmful in the long run, if hostility spills over toward your partner or into your daily work life. Let yourself feel sorry. Know how low you are feeling. And then, in a little bit, get ready to move on, and up.

Purple haze was in my brain,
Lately things don't seem the same.

—*Jimi Hendrix,*
"Purple Haze"

For those of you secretly wondering if the drugs you did in your youth are now coming back to haunt you, rest easy. If you are still dropping acid, you'd be crazy to try and have children now even if you could. But presumably you gave it all up long ago for a more sensible life. There is no scientific evidence to support the vague suspicion that your genes could have been altered along with your mind. If you're a man, anyway, those sperm are long gone. If you are a woman, you are fighting the age of your eggs, not any permanent damage from extracurricular activities of long ago.

You don't live in a world all alone. Your brothers are here too.

—*Albert Schweitzer,*
on receiving the Nobel Prize

✳

Look around you if you have family. Perhaps one or both of your parents are alive. You may have brothers and sisters, close cousins or extended family. Their love for you, as family, has allowed you to grow and make your own life. They nurtured you, and taught you to be your own person and feel confident in yourself.

One day you may provide the same emotional shelter and boost for a family of your own. In the meantime, be thankful for those who reared you. The affection and respect given you is one of the greatest gifts you could have received. Without it, you will not be successful as a parent. With it, you can transmit the gift to your own kids, giving them an incomparable gift as well.

Let there be spaces in your togetherness.
—*Kahlil Gibran,*
The Prophet

Infertility is a very intense experience. In many ways you never could have imagined, it will bring the two of you closer than you ever were before. Wanting to bring children into the world is one of life's most heartfelt decisions and not being able to is one of the most heartbreaking. You can't help but grow closer as you battle the ignominies of the tests and procedures, of doctors too busy to hold your hand or too realistic to build up your hopes. The only person you can really talk to, who really understands the emotional and physical toll this is taking is your spouse.

So be careful. As much as you need to support and rely on each other, you need to respect each other's privacy as well. There will be times when your spouse seems as though he is shutting you out. This is less the case than just a simple need for a little breathing room, a little space.

You don't need to share *all* your waking thoughts with each other; it could be harmful, in fact, if you did. Remember the Prophet and rest easy the next time your spouse just wants to be alone for a while.

Preserve, within a wild sanctuary, an inaccessible valley of reveries.

—*Ellen Glasgow,*
A Certain Measure

*

To keep yourself healthy mentally, you need (among other things) to have an active and personal imaginary life. The ability to daydream about hopes and plans, or just about nonsensical things that make you happy, is vital to your well-being. It's okay not to share every thought you have with someone else. It's okay to nurture dreams and pretend. When your real-life landscape looks a bit too scarred and dangerous, take a few minutes to retreat into your fantasy life. Like jumping into a clear, brilliant stretch of water, the act of withdrawal will refresh and revive you. Or, like opening a familiar and beloved book, it will comfort. Feel free to daydream. It's not a cowardly way out. Quite the opposite—a grown-up "time-out" will help you prioritize, and to sort out what you need in your life. It may just make the difference between a healthy outlook and anxious irritation—and all within the space of under an hour!

May the Force be with you!

—*George Lucas*,
Star Wars

*

Are you fighting the Evil Empire? At times it certainly feels like it. Intuition and instinct are necessarily put aside in favor of methodology and high technology. There seems to be no room for a more thoughtful approach. But this is where you are wrong. It may not appeal to everyone, but I am a firm believer in the power of meditative disciplines such as yoga. If you want the Force to be with you, start doing yoga (or any other mind-body therapy) as often as possible. It doesn't matter what your body type is, or whether you are already in shape or hopelessly unfit. The exercises will strengthen your body, but even better, they will release pent-up stresses and negative tendencies you didn't even know you had. Over time, you'll find that rather than feeling completely out of balance, emotionally and physically, you are gradually becoming more aligned and centered. You'll sleep better at night, and not surprisingly, you'll be able to cope better with the requirements of infertility treatments. Don't just think about it; let the Force be with you.

Why can't a woman be more like a man?

—Alan Jay Lerner,
"Why Can't a Woman,"
My Fair Lady

*

Probably the single greatest stumbling block in rela-
tionships, as far as men are concerned, is the confusion
caused by a woman's acting like a woman, and not like a
man. Men expect women, unrealistically of course, to
think just like men do all the time. Women for their part
seem to expect that men will by some kind of osmosis
understand them clearly and perfectly. The gulf is huge.

Rejoice in your differences. Yes, things get complicated
beyond belief. She said one thing, but she meant *what?*
She assumed you understood what she meant. You
thought your intentions were perfectly clear. It's the old
man-woman story, he said/she said. Well, the very difference between you is what makes your relationship alive
and growing and fun. The tensions that arise, the anxieties, the misunderstandings, can be gotten through with
thought and care. It's wonderful that you both think dif-

ferently. And, if you do eventually have children, it is vital to their well-being. Celebrate that gulf—then try to bridge it with a little kindness, just out of the blue. Surprise her. Make dinner for her, do the laundry, clean the kitchen. Or really surprise her. Agree with her, even when you think she's wrong. You'll surprise yourself.

To live by medicine is to live horribly.

—*Linnaeus,*
Diaeta Naturalis

✳

There is no getting around it. The medical treatment of infertility can be a nasty business, even for the majority of couples who need only low-tech intervention. The tests used to determine if there even is a problem increase in invasiveness as you proceed through them. It's one thing to check the lining of the uterus or have a sperm analysis done, it's another to undergo general anesthesia and abdominal surgery for a laparoscopy. You have to go through *all* of the tests, the doctors say, in order to rule out or pinpoint a problem. Meanwhile you feel violated and confused and wonder if they are right.

Then there's the body-altering world of assisted reproduction—IUI, IVF, GIFT, ZIFT, ICSI. By all accounts of those who have been through it, this is the true horror of reproductive medicine. Daily tests and hormone injections that cause symptoms worse than any bout of PMS and cause your ovaries to swell up like oranges, all for high-tech procedures, some of which are so new they don't need government approval. Many couples feel like guinea pigs but can't give up because giving up would be even worse. Sometimes the technology works, and that's what you keep hoping for.

I have had a good many more uplifting thoughts, creative and expansive visions— while soaking in comfortable baths.

—Edmund Wilson,
A Piece of My Mind

Baths are a no-no, for men at least. Like tight-fitting underwear, warm, and especially hot, baths pose a threat to the temperature your sperm like to form and live in. "Oh come on," you bath lovers might say, but it's true. One case of infertility was solved, quite simply, by eliminating the nightly bedtime bath ritual. So no matter how much you might like to relieve the stress of the day by soaking in a bath, err on the side of caution and give it up. Perky showers only for you, buddy.

Anything awful makes me laugh.

—*Charles Lamb,*
letter to Robert Southey

You have to be able to laugh. Even the simplest case of infertility is god-awful and if you are unable, at least sometimes, to see the black humor in your situation, you're a goner. My husband and I survived on laughter. Not that we happily giggled our way through the entire experience, but we managed to be amused at the absurdity inherent in assisted reproduction. What was horrific at the time would make us laugh later—the semen sample that had to be produced at work, carefully ferried to the clinic via taxi, only to be rejected because the technicians were starting their lunch hour. Imagine an embarrassed and panic-stricken man standing with a naked cup of his precious semen that was only good if it was tested within an hour, pleading with a receptionist who shut the door in his face. The next clinic (I was there, too), with its worn and wrinkled porn magazines, is still good for a chuckle, even five years later, as are the grotesque porn films the female nurse cheerfully and aggressively offered at the clinic doing the insemination. Most important of all, I think, we managed to laugh in bed, when the last thing either of us felt like doing was making babies. If we hadn't been able to laugh and thereby, somehow, get busy, we would have drowned in depression.

In the depth of winter, I finally learned that within me there lay an invincible summer.

—Albert Camus,
"Return to Tipasa,"
Summer

Despair can threaten to overwhelm you. Just as it's difficult to remember in the cold, gray gloom of January that there was ever a soft breeze and a haze of green beyond your back porch, so it is sometimes hard to find hope within the depths of your despair. But you wouldn't have taken up this challenge if you weren't fundamentally optimistic. At your core lies an invincible determination—how else could you keep at it month after month, daunted by the statistical realities, the escalating financial costs, the phone calls from your mother? You are stronger than you give yourself credit; this inner strength, like the summer that follows a long winter, is your salvation.

Faith is the substance of things hoped for, the evidence of things not seen.

—*Hebrews* 11:1

*

If you don't have faith you are lost. Whether it be faith in a higher power, or in the medical technology being offered to you, faith is essential. I have one friend who went through all the tests. She was hopeful after the laparoscopy because sometimes, just by having fluid pushed through your tubes, it can help your chances of becoming pregnant. Her husband underwent surgery to remove tiny varicose veins. They saw one of the best doctors for in-vitro fertilization. But she also visited a psychic and religiously practiced yoga every week. She studied and took herbs. Somewhere along the way (by natural means, not in-vitro), they successfully conceived. She feels strongly it was her willingness to give it up to a higher power, to trust that the baby would come to her, that allowed the pregnancy to happen. Ultimately she had faith, and is very mystical about their child. And by her own account, this would be true even if the pregnancy had occurred through a highly invasive, highly technical procedure such as in-vitro.

*I love the idea of there being two sexes,
don't you?*

—*James Thurber*

*

Reminder: When you first became involved with the
person you now live with, there were just the two of you.
Nowadays, you are practically living with three people—
since the big question, that of The Unborn Child, hangs
over your head day and night. It is slightly ironic that, in
effect, you are now three, not two. In fact, you *are* just
two. Take the time to savor that fact. A couple is a wonderful place to be. Enjoy your mate's difference. Make the
most of it. A raised eyebrow, a sidelong look—and who
knows what that will lead to!

Though patience be a tired mare, yet she will plod.

—William Shakespeare,
Henry V

＊

Sometimes you will feel like an old horse, kicked and prodded and led along the stony path with a bit in your mouth. But like the tired mare, you would do well to plod on. None of us would be able to navigate the world of infertility without patience, and no matter how weary you are, you will be surprised by the depth of your ability to keep on. There is the story of old Job, of course. But I also know of one woman who was finally able to conceive with the help of in-vitro fertilization after *seventeen* years. While you personally might feel that this is too long a time, she felt it was worth it and for her it was. If it helps, think of her the next time you are ready to collapse in the dust.

O world, I cannot hold thee close enough!

—Edna St. Vincent Millay,
"God's World"

*

A quick glance at the headlines in the daily newspaper teaches us that life is fleeting. So often we go through the day without even looking up from our appointments. A sudden event, an accident, a mishap we hear about, always makes us recognize that chance can intervene at any time (the astonishing worldwide reaction to the sudden, tragic death of Princess Diana in a car accident underlines this). It seems, though, that we are consciously grateful for life for only a few moments. Then, robotically, we return to our habits, head down, in our little grooves. Take a break, go outside, look at the view. Take a deep breath and do more than glance at the flowers and trees. Really *see* them. Your existence is precious. Be aware of it, and make the most of it.

There is not a passion so strongly rooted in the human heart as envy.

—*Richard Brinsley Sheridan,*
The Critic

This is especially true for someone who wants desperately to get pregnant. You find yourself envying complete strangers. Worse, you find yourself envying your friends. The differences between you are painfully obvious; they have joined the club and you have not. They either already have their 2.2 children, or they are able to conceive the minute they decide to. Either way, you envy them. No matter how much you love them, no matter how much you think this love should enable you to rise above such a base emotion, you desperately want what they have.

As Sheridan implies, envy is a tenacious passion. There isn't a whole lot to be done except to recognize it for what it is and try to keep a lid on it. Try not to let it get in the way of your friendships. If you find you are avoiding contacting a friend with children, or one who has recently told you she is pregnant, force yourself to make an effort with them. Don't add to your sadness by losing friends.

We shall find peace. We shall hear the angels, we shall see the sky sparkling with diamonds.

—Anton Chekhov,
Uncle Vanya

As hard as it is to believe, there will one day be an end to the struggle. That will be when you are able to come to terms with the fact that life has dealt you a severe setback. It's not easy to accept bad news (and, over time, the news may not be bad after all) but it is essential to do so if you expect to survive as a happy and healthy couple. Things *will* work out, one way or another, but equanimity about it will only come with acceptance of the situation. Yes, you can try to change your luck, and you should. But try to get your mind clear and steady. Read some religious thinkers, Christian or Buddhist or whatever you feel comfortable with. Find a silent place and think quietly, if you want. Try to find peace of mind, which will lead to a peaceful heart.

The beauty of the world has two edges, one of laughter, one of anguish, cutting the heart asunder.

—*Virginia Woolf,*
A Room of One's Own

You will feel as though your heart is breaking at times. Here you are, loving your husband more than you ever thought you could love anyone, loving your life together, profoundly satisfied by the prospect of the future. Perhaps you just bought your first house in anticipation of the family you are planning. And now you're facing the edge of the sword. It amazed me how I could feel such joy one minute and such despair another. That my husband and I could collapse with sorrow, sobbing in the darkness of our bedroom, and suddenly find ourselves turning our anxiety into hope and our tears into laughter. Can you know one without the other? I don't think so. It may be hard to believe, but your anguish will heighten your ability to laugh, and your heartbreak will make your heart grow stronger.

Love is enough, though the world be awaning.

—William Morris,
"Love Is Enough"

We spend a great deal of our day wanting something. It might be as mundane as wanting a new jacket or a new pair of shoes, or our yearning could encompass a much vaster scale: a new job, a more exciting life, a secret fling. This can be a source of guilt, of course, since few of us will move outside the life that we have already created for ourselves. And we often forget that the thing we most want—the love and comfort of another—is right there beside us. Love for one's partner can be an incredibly liberating experience. Beyond the directionless yearning, beyond the need to look for greener pastures, there is one sure and constant force in your life: your mate. Remember why you ended up together. Remember why you chose each other. If you can do so, you'll know that love is indeed enough, and that it can carry you through any form of difficulty you might encounter. At the end of a hard day, it's what will hold you together.

If we are so longing for a child that we are willing to bring up somebody else's child— anybody's child whatever—then we may as well be allowed to have our own.

—William Maxwell,
"The Thistles of Sweden"

*

Adoption is perhaps the thorniest of all options. Most of us can't even think about it, as though doing so is to admit defeat. Most of us know deep down that, of course, it is a distant option, but that we will only go there as a last resort. To decide to adopt is a very different path involving an entirely different mind-set from the course we have been on. Adoption, like infertility, can be extremely difficult, expensive, and time-consuming.

I felt so betrayed when my (fertile) best friend reminded me that "I could always adopt." She was right, theoretically, but it was the last thing on earth I wanted to hear, and the last thing I expected to hear from her. Her gentle suggestion nearly knocked the breath out of me, and I had to hang up the phone immediately. I could barely let myself get angry, so far was I from wanting to even consider adoption. I couldn't think about it and just cried instead.

There are many paths infertile couples take, and adoption can be one, but it's not one you want to discuss until you're ready, if ever. Unlike the couple in Maxwell's short story, some may not want a child if it can't be biologically theirs. Fair enough. Some may decide for whatever reasons that they now are ready to bring up someone else's child as their own. And some couples may bounce in between both ends of the spectrum. For those who for now simply want to be allowed to have a child of their own, adoption is a word better left unsaid.

The end must justify the means.

—Matthew Prior,
Hans Carvel

*

How do you justify the cost, especially when the risk of a pregnancy never occurring looms larger and larger? There are people who have spent $40,000, $50,000, even as much as $100,000 on tests and drugs and high-tech procedures. As if it isn't enough for the emotional costs alone to constantly threaten to overwhelm you, the actual cost certainly will. So *how* do you justify the costs when you don't know when it will end?

Quite simply, only you can decide how far to go if a successful pregnancy is eluding you. The general feeling among those who are still persevering, especially against all odds, is that the possibility of success is more important than the costs. It's worth it, whatever it takes. Such couples need to know that they did everything they could to create a child, and that in the end, the pursuit of this goal should leave them with no regrets. Even if you need to stop before you've conceived, at least you will know you've taken it as far as you are able.

Are we having fun yet?

—*Bill Griffith*,
Zippy the Pinhead

✳

Nope, we're not. But this is an awfully good line to use when you're feeling particularly beleaguered. Try it the next time you and your spouse are waiting in some clinic, dealing with an unhappy-looking technician to whom you would not trust your car let alone your reproductive fluid. Or in bed when you are facing the fourth consecutive night of reproductive activity (if four nights in a row doesn't sound like much, you're a newcomer). Or when, like a squirrel hiding nuts for the winter, you find yourself cleaning out sock drawers or shelves in the refrigerator to store your injectibles. As I've mentioned before, humor will be your salvation.

Time for a little something.

—A. A. Milne,
Winnie-the-Pooh

*

Pooh knew when it was time to have a little honey from his honey-jar, and you should too. As you get caught up in the obsession of trying to get pregnant, remember to take time out for yourself and do something special. You have been immersed in the pregnancy issue to the boiling point; you've been going through all the paces, doing everything when you should and how you should; you've been patient (with your mate and with yourself). But there does come a point when you need to escape, even if briefly, and do something for yourself that has nothing to do with your home life. For instance, you might take a two-day trip up to Maine to the L.L. Bean fishing school, if that is something that has ever appealed to you. Or you might just treat yourself to that restaurant you've always wanted to try. Or maybe take a day to go see some movies. Whatever you end up doing, you do need to do those little (or big) things that will make you feel connected with the world and with yourself in a way you haven't felt for a while. While getting pregnant is the primary issue in your life right now, there's a whole other side to your life that is vital and important and that you need to cultivate. So feel free, as soon as you can, to indulge.

The excursion is the same when you go looking for your sorrow as when you go looking for your joy.

—Eudora Welty,
"The Wide Net"

＊

You can't help but think that your life would be great if only you were pregnant. You imagine that everything would be different, joyful, and of course, in many ways it would. But it is also true that the sorrow you experience every day you fail to conceive does not fundamentally change who you are and what your life is. You perceive it as such; everyone imagines the grass is greener regardless of the problems they face. Having a child will bring you endless joy, yes, but in your quest to reach that goal, don't overlook the importance of the journey along the way. The path you are now on is full of invaluable life lessons.

People love to say that God gives you only as much as you can handle. If you are like most people facing infertility, such a comment will only serve to make you angry. Go ahead, get angry, but don't prevent yourself from learning from it, too. Your anger can be your strength, as can your ability to incorporate your experiences with infertility into your life.

Doubts are more cruel than the worst of truths.

—Molière,
The Misanthrope

You might think the worst thing you could find out is that you absolutely cannot have children of your own. But often the finality of the truth, when you hear it, is easier to reconcile than your doubts. Those couples who can't ever conceive usually go on to adopt their children, and are happy having done so. But those who can conceive, or who are still hoping they can conceive, but haven't yet, can exist in a purgatory of doubt.

Before you beat yourself up too much with your doubts, consider this: Doubts are normal. You can't possibly keep your hopes up all the time. Cruel as your doubts might be, having them does not mean they are going to come true, either. I think it's easy to become superstitious, and that's fine as long as you can laugh about it. But when your doubts threaten to overwhelm you and you can't shrug them off, make yourself consider what exactly you fear—

that you will never be a Dad? That you will never play ball with a son or daughter? Well, maybe not, to be honest. But if that proves to be the case, at least you can begin to come to grips with the truth, and direct your life accordingly. Scant comfort—but believe me, swallowing the bitter pill of reality will make you better equipped for daily life than constantly wrestling with doubt.

Fortunately analysis is not the only way to re-solve inner conflicts. Life itself still remains a very effective therapist.

—Karen Horney,
Our Inner Conflicts

★

This is both true and not true. For some couples, facing the difficulties of infertility brings them closer together. I know of one couple whose marriage was consistently rocky until they started trying to get pregnant. When it didn't happen and didn't happen and the woman had to undergo surgery as well as hormone treatments, their relationship got better and better. They hadn't been working toward the same goals before, but when they got down to a fundamental level, they were there for each other. Their relationship became much more honest and loving and secure. Now they are the proud parents of twins.

On the other hand, some marriages, no matter how strong, wouldn't survive the trials of infertility without the help of psychotherapy. Not being able to conceive can precipitate a monumental personal crisis, which in turn threatens the marriage. As time wears on, and success seems ever more elusive, the strain can become too much for even the most supportive couples. Consider just some of the issues: You constantly feel like a failure, the treatments and procedures are deeply invasive, both physically and spiritually, and the costs threaten to bury your future. Not that the added cost of a therapist is what you need either, but by all accounts, it's worth it. If you think you might need help, you do. Get counseling as soon as possible.

A single gentle rain makes the grass many shades greener. So our prospects brighten on the influx of better thoughts.

—Henry David Thoreau,
Walden

✳

Many truths can be found in the observations of the great cranky Thoreau, but this one, written as spring was emerging from the cold depths of a New England winter, is particularly heartening. How often do we "loiter in winter while it is already spring," as he goes on to write? Just as grass can grow noticeably greener after just one warm spring rain, so we, too, can alter our state of mind by a little positive thinking, by living in the present rather than lingering in the past or worrying about the future. Nature is constantly changing, renewing itself, dying away, only to come back with increased vigor and beauty. It's been said many times, by many different people in many different ways, but the voice of nature *is* encouraging. We have only to take the time to listen to take heart.

My punishment is greater than I can bear.

—*Genesis 4:13*

*

We all carry our own crosses and so it's difficult to say just what is the hardest punishment to bear. But for many, a miscarriage is a true heartbreak. Even for fertile couples miscarriages are not uncommon within the first twelve weeks of a pregnancy, but for infertile couples the percentages are higher. And the stakes are higher, too. To try so hard for so long, to hope and pray and pay and then, as last, to have your deepest wish fulfilled by a simple blood test—the euphoria is hard to describe. And so is the devastation when that tiny heart on the sonogram screen has suddenly, inexplicably, stopped beating. And for those who lose more than several (after three miscarriages, the general consensus suggests that you see a specialist); or lose a pregnancy at a later stage, at eighteen weeks when you are finally starting to relax; or worse, at eight months, just as you think you've made it to the magical thirty-two weeks—well the pain and sadness is simply unbearable.

But somehow we do bear it, and ultimately are comforted by the fact that the miracle happened at all, even for a limited time. We start trying again, and listen hard to all the stories about how women often get pregnant following a miscarriage. They do, and you will too.

*For thy sake, Tobacco, I
Would do anything but die.*

—*Charles Lamb*,
"A Farewell to Tobacco"

*

One last word about the smoking issue. As a former smoker (fifteen years at a couple of packs of nonfilters a day), I know how great smoking can be. I used to love smoking. I loved everything about it: the smoke, the sound of the matches, the feel of the pack, the feeling of that first puff curling up into my lungs. Quitting, which I did one Sunday morning after waking up from a dream in which I quit and then felt miraculously healthy and happy, was the hardest thing I've ever done. Forget the moral overtones so many people use against smoking and for quitting. Morality has nothing to do with it. In your case, we're talking sperm count. And basic health. Yes, it *is* true that nonsmokers, and men who have even recently quit, have a much higher sperm count than smokers. Their chances for conception are far, far greater, all other things being equal. If you are serious about wanting to have a child, and if you are putting yourself through the paces in other ways (taking the tests, eating better), then do this too. Quit now. Within days, your sperm count will be higher. Quit now.

What else is there to say but everything?
—Gwendolyn Brooks,
"In the Mecca"

So much more could be offered to help you through this difficult phase of your life, but ultimately you must find your own best way to cope with the inevitable ups and downs. If these quotes and thoughts have helped you in any way, then they have done their job. So much of the battle against infertility is a heartless process, but perhaps now you can take heart with a little more confidence, or at least the knowledge that you are not the only one who feels a certain way.

Resources and Further Reading

RESOLVE, 1310 Broadway, Somerville, Massachusetts 02144, (617) 623-0744, www.resolve.org. This is a nationwide organization (founded in 1974) dedicated to providing compassionate support and information to those experiencing infertility. Support groups are run in cities across the country.

alt.infertility is an Internet news group for people coping with a variety of issues and stages of infertility. The postings can be highly personal and can provide comfort and support as well as shared information. The Internet can be an especially valuable resource for those wishing for anonymity.

Society for Assisted Reproductive Technology, Birmingham, Alabama, (205) 978-5000, can provide information on a member clinic's credentials and success rates. They can supply (for a fee) a report on clinics in your area.

There are dozens, if not hundreds, of books available to you for further reading about the subject of infertility. Your local library is sure to stock some of them. Any titles you don't see on the shelves there are easily gotten through interlibrary loan, at no cost to you. Of course, be sure to check with your local bookstore too; they will be more than happy to special order any book they don't already stock. Even if you don't know specific titles, you can browse through library catalogs, or on the Internet, looking under subject headings such as "infertility," "sexuality," "childbirth," "parenting," and other key phrases.

What follows is a list of books that cover some of the topics mentioned in our book. This is far from comprehensive, but it does give you a place to start. We hope you find something here that will help answer your questions.

The American Medical Women's Association Guide to Fertility and Reproductive Health by Roselyn Payne, M.D., and Susan Cobb, M.D. Dell, 1996, $4.99.

The Complete Guide to Fertility and Family Planning by Sarah Freeman and Vern L. Bullough. Prometheus Books, 1993, $16.95.

Conceptions and Misconceptions: The Informed Patient's Guide to In-vitro and Other Assisted Reproduction Methods by Arthur L. Wisat and David Meldrum. Hartley & Marks, 1997, $19.95.

The Couples' Guide to Fertility: Techniques to Help You Have a Baby by Gary Berger, Marc Goldstein, and Mark Fuerst. Main Street Books, 1995, $16.95.

Dr. Richard Marr's Fertility Book: America's Leading Fertility Expert Tells You Everything You Need to Know About Getting Pregnant by Richard Marr, M.D.,

Lisa Friedman Bloch, and Kathy Kirtland Silverman. Delacorte Press, 1997, $25.95.

50 Essential Things to Do When the Doctors Say It's Infertility by B. Blake Levitt. Plume, 1995, $10.95.

Getting Pregnant: What Couples Need to Know Right Now by Neils H. Laverson and Colette Bouchoz. Fawcett Books, 1992, $12.95.

Getting Pregnant When You Thought You Couldn't: The Interactive Guide That helps You Up the Odds by Helane S. Rosenberg and Yakov M. Epstein. Warner Books, 1993, $13.99.

How to be a Successful Fertility Patient: Your Guide to Getting the Best Possible Medical Help to Have a Baby by Peggy Robin. Quill, 1993, $15.

Infertility: Your Questions Answered by S. L. Tan et al. Citadel Press, 1997, $14.95.

The Language of Fertility: A Revolutionary Mind-Body Program for Conscious Consumption by Niravi B. Payne and Brenda Lane Richardson. Random House, 1997, $25.

Overcoming Infertility: 12 Couples Share Their Success Stories by Herbert A. Goldfarb et al. John Wiley & Sons, 1995, $14.95.

Overcoming Infertility: A Compassionate Resource for Getting Pregnant by Robert Jansen. W. H. Freeman & Co., 1997, $24.95.

Sweet Grapes: How to Stop Being Infertile and Start Living Again by Jean W. Carter. Perspectives Press, 1991, $12.

Taking Charge of Infertility: Essential Facts and Up-to-the-Minute Information on the Techniques and Treatments to Achieve Pregnancy by Susan Treiser and Robin K. Levinson. Hyperion, 1994, $9.95.

FOR THE BEST IN PAPERBACKS, LOOK FOR THE

In every corner of the world, on every subject under the sun, Penguin represents quality and variety—the very best in publishing today.

For complete information about books available from Penguin—including Puffins, Penguin Classics, and Arkana—and how to order them, write to us at the appropriate address below. Please note that for copyright reasons the selection of books varies from country to country.

In the United Kingdom: Please write to *Dept. JC, Penguin Books Ltd, FREEPOST, West Drayton, Middlesex UB7 0BR*.

If you have any difficulty in obtaining a title, please send your order with the correct money, plus ten percent for postage and packaging, to *P.O. Box No. 11, West Drayton, Middlesex UB7 0BR*

In the United States: Please write to *Consumer Sales, Penguin USA, P.O. Box 999, Dept. 17109, Bergenfield, New Jersey 07621-0120*. VISA and MasterCard holders call 1-800-253-6476 to order all Penguin titles

In Canada: Please write to *Penguin Books Canada Ltd, 10 Alcorn Avenue, Suite 300, Toronto, Ontario M4V 3B2*

In Australia: Please write to *Penguin Books Australia Ltd, P.O. Box 257, Ringwood, Victoria 3134*

In New Zealand: Please write to *Penguin Books (NZ) Ltd, Private Bag 102902, North Shore Mail Centre, Auckland 10*

In India: Please write to *Penguin Books India Pvt Ltd, 706 Eros Apartments, 56 Nehru Place, New Delhi 110 019*

In the Netherlands: Please write to *Penguin Books Netherlands bv, Postbus 3507, NL-1001 AH Amsterdam*

In Germany: Please write to *Penguin Books Deutschland GmbH, Metzlerstrasse 26, 60594 Frankfurt am Main*

In Spain: Please write to *Penguin Books S.A., Bravo Murillo 19, 1° B, 28015 Madrid*

In Italy: Please write to *Penguin Italia s.r.l., Via Felice Casati 20, I-20124 Milano*

In France: Please write to *Penguin France S.A., 17 rue Lejeune, F-31000 Toulouse*

In Japan: Please write to *Penguin Books Japan, Ishikiribashi Building, 2-5-4, Suido, Bunkyo-ku, Tokyo 112*

In Greece: Please write to *Penguin Hellas Ltd, Dimocritou 3, GR-106 71 Athens*

In South Africa: Please write to *Longman Penguin Southern Africa (Pty) Ltd, Private Bag X08, Bertsham 2013*